Don't Look Back!

A 21 Day Devotional

Leila Williams

Copyright © 2021 Leila Williams

All rights reserved. No part of this book may be reproduced in any form or by any electronic or mechanical means, including information storage and retrieval systems, without permission in writing from the publisher, except by reviewers, who may quote brief passages in a review.

ISBN: 978-1-955312-06-6
Printed in the United States of America

Story Corner Publishing & Consulting, Inc.
1510 Atlanta Ave.
Portsmouth, VA 23704
Storycornerpublishing@yahoo.com
www.StoryCornerPublishing.com

Dedication

I want to dedicate this book to everyone who supported me and walked me through my many journeys. To my family, I love each of you and you will always have a place in my heart. To my dearest church family, Open Heart Deliverance Ministry, I love you also. You all have been riding with me for years and I thank you.

I also want to dedicate this book to everyone who thought they could not make it. I want to encourage you that you can do all things through Jesus Christ. You just have to believe. Don't focus on yesterday but look forward to today.

Table of Content

Introduction

Day 1: The Hands That Protected Me Was the Hands That Hurt Me

Day 2: Crying Makes You Ugly

Day 3: No Longer A Slave to My YES

Day 4: Discovering Your True Self

Day 5: Stand Up: Women Are Not Second-Class Citizens

Day 6: Why So Many Kids? Because the Bible Said So!

Day 7: I Didn't Know Him Like I Pretended I Did

Day 8: Sacrificing for The Wrong Person

Day 9: Self-Abuse Has Taken Over Me

Day 10: I Know My Worth

Day 11: The Place That Tried to Assassinate Me

Day 12: There Are Two of Me

Day 13: When Your Leader Can't Hear God for You

Day 14: Loneness Verses Being Alone

Day 15: If You Judge It, You Will Become It

Day 16: I Am A Perfectionist, And It Drives Me Crazy

Day 17: The Healing Begins Now

Day 18: Location Is Everything

Day 19: The Why Over the What

Day 20: I AM Free

Day 21: You Are A Survivor

Introduction

Have you ever felt lost, confused, or lonely? Well, this is the devotional for you. This is not the typical or ordinary prayer devotional either. This book covers real-life everyday topics and gives you hope to make it through the process. There is strength when we wait on The Lord. I have enclosed the necessary tools to accomplish the process, my testimonies, and an "elimination station" section where you have the opportunity to leave all the toxins behind as you write then out. Please do not bypass utilizing the "elimination station" section to write your thoughts, emotions, testimony, prayers, notes, etc. Freedom is just one page and one release away.

Day 1

The Hands That Protected Me Was the Hands That Hurt Me

Scripture: "So in everything, do to others what you would have them do to you, for this sums up the Law and the Prophets." *Matthew 7:12 NIV*

Testimony:

As a child, you should not have to worry about too much of anything. The child should have their needs met and feel safe. Usually, these things are the responsibilities of one's family. What happens when the child does not feel safe at home? Home should be the safe haven set apart from the world, but for me, it was not. I was touched inappropriately as a child. My innocence was taken away by one of the ones that were supposed to be protecting me. They saved me from everyone one else, so I could not understand why they would hurt me. These same hands that would fight for me took advantage of me. They did me wrong, and for so long, I was mentally stuck in the cycle of abuse. I thought I was dirty, and no one would ever genuinely love me.

I got older and began to do others wrong. I treated people dirty even if they came to help me because I still had the mindset that I was dirty. I figured I would treat them this way before they treated me dirty. The abuse from my childhood made me walk in embarrassment and shame. When you walk in shame, you walk in remain. Things will stay the same if your perspective does not change.

It took me to accept a real relationship with Jesus Christ to overcome my past. He helped me to deal with the shame instead of sweeping it under the rug. I could no longer hide from it. Once I dealt with the guilt, I was delivered out of the darkness. I was set free from the mental prison that drove me crazy at times. Don't allow an event to become a series in your life. Allow Jesus to break you free from the chains!

Prayer:

Dear Lord,

Help Your people to be bold in You and to overcome fear and shame. Cleanse away the abuse and reset their mind in you. Help them to know that You love them in Jesus's/ Yeshua's name, Amen.

Elimination Station:

_____
_____
_____
_____
_____
_____
_____
_____

Day 2

Crying Makes You Ugly

<u>Scripture:</u> "I praise you because I am fearfully and wonderfully made; your works are wonderful, I know that full well." **Psalms 139:14 NIV**

Testimony:

My parents told me not to cry because it made me look ugly. I guess their intentions were good, but they did not realize what seeds they were planting. I felt that if I expressed my emotions, people would think that I was ugly. Coming from a family that did not affirm me only made me work extra hard to gain their affection. My parents were not the type to hug and give compliments. I wanted to make them proud because I believed one day they would change. They said not to cry, so I didn't. I held in my emotions until one day, I could not control them anymore. They began to control me. I could not understand why I became so sad, miserable, and depressed. I hid this for a long time because I did not want to disappoint my parents. Others around me began to see a change in me, but I did not know how to form it all into words.

I found myself turning to God in prayer. God began to reveal who He is to me and who I am to Him. God assured me that I was perfect because He created me, that was. No more did I have to hold back in order to please others. When I began to allow myself to cry, I felt an immediate release! All this time, I fought to keep my tears in, not realizing that they were the very thing that would free me from the misery that came over me. After I cried and cried some more, I felt more beautiful than I have ever felt in my life!

When people act out, we tend to look at the "what" instead of the "why." We look at what they do and what they say because there is always a reason to respond this way. Never judge a book by its cover. Love on everyone because you never know what they could be going through or have been through in their lives.

Prayer:

Heavenly Father,

Despite what people say, please help us to hold on to what you said. Grace us to grace others. Please help us to shed beautiful tears so we can live a healthy and whole life in you in Jesus's/ Yeshua's name, Amen.

Elimination Station:

_____
_____
_____
_____
_____
_____
_____
_____

Day 3

No Longer A Slave to My YES

Scripture: "Love is patient, love is kind. It does not envy, it does not boast, it is not proud. It does not dishonor others, it is not self-seeking, it is not easily angered, it keeps no record of wrongs. Love does not delight in evil but rejoices with the truth. It always protects, always trusts, always hopes, always perseveres. Love never fails…" *1 Corinthians 13:4-8 NIV*

Testimony:

Sometimes we find ourselves doing so much for others that we lose ourselves. We tend to juggle so much that it is unnecessary in life that we forget about the assignments we are called to do. We rush to the aid of others and even drop everything for them, but what happens when you do not get the same in return? You help others to get their lives in order. You push others to perfection, and then you look around, and no one is there when you need a push. We invest time, money, advice, resources, etc., and sometimes do not even get a simple "thank you." I grew bitter and felt like I was a prisoner to my YES. I did not know how to say NO and could not understand why. I wanted to do better with prioritizing my YES, but I felt that I would be letting others down that really needed me.

Just know when it comes to God, He will never make you feel this way. He loves us beyond words and wants the best for every last one of us. His love is not selfish, and He is always quick to give of Himself. Jesus came into this world not to be served but to serve. This understanding helped me to get past the fact that everyone will not give themselves to me as I give to them. Just because I do a thing does not mean others will follow the same. I overcame disappointment that plagued me for years. I had to allow God to change my perspective on giving of myself. When we walk in God's love, we must selflessly give of ourselves just as Jesus did. I am simply happy that I had and still have something to bring to someone else's life. Place your YES in God's hands and allow Him to guild you to the people who need your service.

Prayer:

Lord,

Please step in and change the minds and perspectives of your people. Show us how to selflessly serve others according to your will for their lives. Show us who we are called to and who to lead back to you in Jesus's/ Yeshua's name, Amen.

Elimination Station:

_____
_____
_____
_____
_____
_____
_____
_____

Day 4

Discovering My True Self

Scripture: "I can do all this through him who gives me strength."
Philippians 4:13 NIV

Testimony:

For so long, I was labeled with the symbol of the scarlet letter "A" for Adultery. I committed a sin that followed for years. I asked for forgiveness and even tried to make it right, only to be shown no mercy. I know it was wrong of me, but how long was I going to pay for it? The Word of God tells us that God will forgive us as we forgive others. Forgiveness should be something that we put into practice every day. Since no one seemed to forgive me, I began to think that Adultery was who I was and all I would ever be.

God reminded me of the story in the Bible of the women caught in the act of adultery. He illuminated the part when Jesus said to the people, "He who is without sin cast the first stone." No one threw a stone because they all have sinned. Then Jesus told the woman to go in peace and sin no more. This opened my eyes and brought me great comfort because Jesus never referred to her as the adulterer but as a woman. The same title that He referred to His mother Mary. "Woman," back then was a form of respect. In no way did Jesus disrespect the woman that was caught in the act of adultery. No matter how messy the situation was He showed her compassion. All this time, I allowed the people to tell me who I was, but today I know that I am a woman. I am a woman who fell short of God's glory back then but has been forgiven. I am also and have always been a child of God who is loved by Him very much. Whose report are you going to believe?

Prayer:

Dear Lord,

Deliver your people from the opinions of others and help them to know you love them unconditionally no matter what. Remind your people who they are to you in Jesus's/ Yeshua's name, Amen.

Elimination Station:

_____
_____
_____
_____
_____
_____
_____
_____

Day 5

Stand Up:
Women Are Not Second-Class Citizens

Scripture: "Therefore put on the full armor of God, so that when the day of evil comes, you may be able to stand your ground, and after you have done everything, to stand." ***Ephesians 6:13 NIV***

Testimony:

Being a female is tough sometimes because we are overlooked. Many think we cannot do certain things and should not do certain things. Women experience so many closed doors and must fight twice as hard as men just to be heard. In ministry, we are taught that women are to sit and be quiet. We can sit in the front row if we look beautiful and do not have an opinion about anything. We are to smile and wave. Truly dead on the inside, but glamorous on the outside. The Word of God tells us that God poured His Spirit out on ALL flesh, Sons, and Daughters. Therefore, we are ALL assigned by God to fulfill a purpose, and it will not get done sitting down or being quiet.

Once I finally took a stand, I realized that women were called as well. We can do just as much work, if not better. I am not saying women should take over, but for men and society to move over and make room for us. There is work to be done. Men cannot do it all alone, even though they think they can. We, as women, were created to be a helpmeet. Women are the help that is tailor-made to stand by the man.

We are not slaves, doormats, or second-class citizens. We are equals and not less than. Ladies, it is time to take a stand! No longer allow the world to take your voice away because you have something the world needs to hear. Know who you are and whose you are. You are a Daughter of THE KING!

Prayer:

Father God,

Please help your daughters to take a stand in confidence. Let them know you need them as well. Take away fear, doubt, and stress in Jesus's/ Yeshua's name, Amen.

Elimination Station:

_____
_____
_____
_____
_____
_____
_____
_____
_____

Day 6

Why So Many Kids? Because the Bible Said So!

Scripture: "Blessed is the man whose quiver is full of them. They will not be put to shame when they contend with their opponents in court." **Psalms 127:5 NIV**

Testimony:

For so long, people made me feel ashamed of myself once they heard how many children I have. They would laugh, call me crazy, and tell me I was stupid to have so many children. They would want to know how I was providing for all of them. They wanted to know how I stayed sane with all of them running around, but I never looked at my children with that mindset. I would always wonder why my children were the conversation in the first place. I was never trying to hide my children or ashamed of them, but I was ashamed of myself. I thought I did something wrong. At one point, I started to believe that having children was wrong, although I was married. Society will have you think you have to fit into a mold and look like everyone else. That was never me, so I never fit in even when I tried. Believe me, I tried many times only to stand out still!

Scripture is always true, and it tells us that the fruit of the womb is blessed. Children are blessings no matter what people say. The Bible tells us to be fruitful, multiply, and subdue the earth. People in the Bible days honored being able to have children. Hence why most of them gave birth to tribes of children. They knew children carry the legacy on, and if there are no children, the legacy dies. I know I was called to birth nations, and not everyone is purposed to do so.

Today, I am freer than I have ever been! I know that I have fulfilled my purpose of birthing generations that will rise above the world's view and declaring the works of the Lord. I am free from the box of people's thoughts of me. Once you lay down what the people say and hold onto what God say, you too will be FREE! Choose God because He knows what's best.

Prayer:

Father,

Deliver your people from judging things they do not understand. Please help them to embrace one another and be more supportive in Jesus's/ Yeshua's name, Amen.

Elimination Station:

_____
_____
_____
_____
_____
_____
_____
_____

Day 7

I Didn't Know Him Like I Pretended I Did

Scripture: "I want to know Christ—yes, to know the power of his resurrection and participation in his sufferings, becoming like him in his death," ***Philippians 3:10 NIV***

Testimony:

I was born and raised in the church. The church was all I have ever known. I knew the ends and outs of running a service, collecting the money, jumping around, dancing, and even crying on cue when service elevated with excitement. I learned all of this because it was what I saw each and every week. I began to imitate what I saw, and the rest was history. After years of this, I realized everyone was the same with nothing new to show for all the time we spent in church.

Shouldn't there be a newness that takes over us at some point? The Word of God tells me we are new in Jesus Christ. Isn't the church the location to find Jesus? Or is it not? I started to have so many questions. Once I started seeking God in prayer for answers, He showed up and transitioned my mind from "church" to "Christ." I realized all this time I knew the church, but not God. That was the reason change was not evident! I thought I was losing my mind some days, but I continued to go to church because that's what they said to do. Nothing wrong with the church, but when you do not have a real relationship with God first, you will get lost. I felt stuck locked away on a Ferris wheel going round and round but getting nowhere.

When God steps into your life, it is EVIDENT! No question about it. After God introduced Himself to me, I could NOT go back to my old ways. I was changed, so there was nothing even to go back to. I began scanning the room everywhere I went to weed out the real from the fake. Know that only God can introduce Himself to you, and you have to want it. One encounter with Him, and the act is over. He is calling for a real relationship with all of us. Are you ready?

Prayer:

Father God,

Please reveal yourself and your power to me. I want to know you for real. I do not want to pretend any longer in Jesus's/ Yeshua's name, Amen.

Elimination Station:

_____
_____
_____
_____
_____
_____
_____
_____

Day 8

Sacrificing for The Wrong Person

Scripture: He told her, "Go, call your husband and come back." "I have no husband," she replied. Jesus said to her, "You are right when you say you have no husband. The fact is, you have had five husbands, and the man you now have is not your husband. What you have just said is quite true." ***John 4:16-18 NIV***

Testimony:

I used to wonder why the one I loved did not love me the same. I would go over and beyond for them. Whatever they needed, I was there to give. If I did not have it to offer, I would find it to give. I would notice that the ones I loved always had their hands out for me to pour into them, but they would never come with anything in their hands to give. This cycle went on for years in my life with different people, but the same treatment. I would feel like I was caught up in the same scene of life but a different cast. I longed for things to change. Until then, I continued to give all of me.

One day I realized I was not happy. I felt empty and bitter. I had created a void within that I could not fulfill. No matter how I tried to change this, I failed every time. I had nothing else to give. I was drained dry!

How could I ever be replenished? The only thing I could think of in my moment of desperation was to call on Jesus. I needed a savior, and I needed Him to come quick. Jesus is the only one who can quench your thirst. He is the one who fulfills our voids and brings us out of whatever depleted state we find ourselves. Ask the Lord to show you who to sacrifice for because not everyone deserves you.

Prayer:

Father God,

Please help us to be okay with waiting on who you want to connect with us. Remove anxiousness, worry, and stress. Fine-tune our ears and eyes to be about to recognize when the one you sent is in front of us in Jesus's/ Yeshua's name, Amen.

Elimination Station:

_____
_____
_____
_____
_____
_____
_____
_____

Day 9

Self-Abuse Has Taken Over Me

Scripture: "O my love, you are altogether beautiful and fair. There is no flaw nor blemish in you!"
Song of Solomon 4:7 AMP

Testimony:

Every morning I wake up, I look in the mirror. Some days I like what I see, and some days I don't. Lately, I have been finding more and more flaws. I sometimes wonder how I see things I'm not too fond of today that I did not see yesterday. It's like, my imperfections are taking over.

I leave the house for work, school, etc., and I fall into this routine of comparing myself to everything and everyone around me. I cannot even read a magazine or watch a T.V show without comparing myself and my life. It seems like every woman on the screen or in the magazines is beautiful and well put together. They always have a great life, great body, great guy, great car, great friends, etc.

Every time I look in the mirror, I ask God what happen to me? Why don't I have "great" everything? I began to believe imperfections were all I was suitable for. I started to think that I was ugly and never going to be good enough. I would find myself crying every time I looked into the mirror until one day, I just stopped. I thought nothing would ever change anyway, so why keep looking?

I never knew this was the enemy feeding these thoughts to my mind until God answered my cry. God reminded me that I was His creation and everything He created is good no matter if I feel good about myself or not. God also let me know that He did not make mistakes in anything He does, even how He created me. I could not thank God enough for simply creating me. We tend to lose sight of what's essential when saturated with so much fluff around us. Remember, you are beautiful no matter what they say or how you feel some days!

Prayer:

Dear Lord,

I thank you for creating us in your perfect image. I pray that we will remember that even when we do not feel our best. Please continue to wrap your arms around us when our mind starts to wander in Jesus's/ Yeshua's name, Amen.

Elimination Station:

_____
_____
_____
_____
_____
_____
_____
_____

Day 10

I Know My Worth

Scripture: "An excellent woman [one who is spiritual, capable, intelligent, and virtuous], who is he who can find her? Her value is more precious than jewels and her worth is far above rubies or pearls." ***Proverbs 31:10***

Testimony:

Rubies are one of the rarest precious gems in the world. They stand in a class alone. Often, they are priced higher than diamonds. Rubies are distinct in color and worn as luxury items. Biblically, rubies represent beauty and wisdom.

No matter where rubies are located or who possesses them, the value of the gem never decreases. Knowing that we are the children of The Most High God, our value will never diminish. God has given us power, love, and a sound mind which is far better than rubies. God has invested in us, so never think lightly of yourself. He also gave up His only son so that we could be saved. His investment paid it all for us. We are dear to His heart, and He would do it a billion more times to show us how much we mean to Him.

Prayer:

Holy Father,

Thank you for the value you have added to our lives. Please help us always to remember our worth because we belong to you in Jesus's/ Yeshua's name, Amen.

Elimination Station:

Day 11
The Place That Tried to Assassinate Me

Scripture: Not at all! Let God be true, and every human being a liar. As it is written: "So that you may be proved right when you speak and prevail when you judge." **Romans 3:4 NIV**

Testimony:

I remember being a young teenager and in a relationship. I knew it was time to let him go, but I still loved him. I moved on after a few months and met someone else. I got married thinking it was the right thing to do, but the thoughts of my old relationship would haunt me. I felt after I moved on and even got married the love, I had for my ex would die. Instead, the feelings that I had for him only grew out of control. After a while, he was all I thought about. I happened to run into him in the neighborhood not too long after he and I broke up. I couldn't believe he was standing in front of me after I told myself I never wanted to see him again. My heart was racing, and all I could think about was the good times we spent together. One thing led to another, we got alone, and I gave myself to him. At that moment, it was great, but after we were done, I immediately felt shame and guilt come over me. I was still married and had no business even talking to my ex.

I cheated on my husband without even considering how he would feel. I was selfish, and I knew this could not go on any longer with my ex. I told him goodbye and came clean with my husband. I thought he would have wanted a divorce, but instead, he showed me mercy and forgave me over time. In the meantime, I cried out to the church asking for help because I did not want to slip again. Instead of the church helping me, they exposed me, crucified me, and labeled me! They would preach about me in their sermons and have convinced everyone to protect their husbands so I wouldn't take them away. They labeled me as an adulterer, unclean, and unholy. For 22 years, I went to this church that only put me down and gossiped about me. I went through emotional and mental trauma at the hand of the church.

The church building is supposed to be a hospital, a school, and a safe place. The people are supposed to heal the sick and teach others the gospel of Jesus Christ so they can share it with someone else. The church failed me when I needed help the most. Since then, God stepped in and did perfect work in me. He took the desire of lust away from me and helped me to be the wife I needed to be. I forgave the church and have moved on with life. I did not want God chastising me for holding unforgiveness in my heart. God's Word tell us to forgive others when they do us wrong so God can forgive us. I need God to forgive me everyday, so I knew I had to forgive them. God really changed me and I am grateful for it. God even relocated me to another church that was more supportive of my needs going forward. When you let go of the hurt and pain, God can step in and began the healing process. Release everything to God no matter how hard it may seem and watch your life shift.

Prayer:

Dear Lord,

I pray that you cover all of your people. I pray when the system fails them, you are there to help them up continue on. Please comfort all of those who went through abuse in Jesus's/ Yeshua's name, Amen.

Elimination Station:

_____
_____
_____
_____
_____
_____
_____
_____

Day 12

There Is Two of Me

Scripture: "For in my inner being I delight in God's law; but I see another law at work in me, waging war against the law of my mind and making me a prisoner of the law of sin at work within me." ***Romans 7:22-23 NIV***

Testimony:

When I became a believer in Jesus Christ, my mindset changed to do good. I realized my old character would conflict with my anointing. It was a fight to do right and not go back to my old ways. I would sometimes doubt my salvation because of the struggle I had within. I knew I loved Jesus with my whole heart, but why was it so hard to do right at times? Once I started to mature in my salvation, I understood that there are levels to all of this. Sometimes we could be in a struggle not knowing we need deliverance. We could be just set apart from the temptation with no real test, but once the temptation appears, we would know where we stand in our deliverance process. Or we could be delivered, and that chapter has closed in our lives. Either way, we all must go through our process in life to achieve deliverance. We have to be honest with the level we stand on so we can know how to pray or go about seeking God for help. When we fully allow God to reset us to the settings in which He created us, we will become free and able to face anything.

Prayer:

Father God,

I chose to surrender everything to you, including myself. I need your help and guidance to become a better me. Without you, I can not make it. Help us all to trust you more in Jesus's/ Yeshua's name, Amen.

Elimination Station:

_____
_____
_____
_____
_____
_____
_____
_____

Day 13

When Your Leader Can't Hear God for You

Scripture: "And he ran to Eli and said, "Here I am; you called me." But Eli said, "I did not call; go back and lie down." So he went and lay down." *1 Samuel 3:5 NIV*

Testimony:

When I accepted salvation, God encountered me in a way that I had never imagined. I could hear God's voice and really feel Him. Before salvation, I would try to read scripture and would either fall asleep or did not understand what I read. It was like I was cut off from understanding God. Salvation granted me access to another world. The spirit realm where God lives is open to everyone, but you have to tap in. We must seek God so we can build a relationship with Him in order to tap into His space.

No longer do we have to sit and entirely rely on the spiritual leaders to tell us what God is saying. God wants to speak to each of us because we are His creation, His sheep. Scripture tells us His sheep knows His voice. How can we know His voice if He is not speaking? God speaks every day through everything. We must settle ourselves and listen. God does not want us to become lazy or complacent to the point we look at our spiritual leaders as God. God is a jealous God, and He will share His glory with no one! God wants us to seek Him for answers because He is The All-Knowing One. Our spiritual leaders only see in part. They will never see the whole picture for our lives and could lead us astray if we are not careful. So, seek God for all of your answers and direction because He knows the way.

Prayer:

Heavenly Father,

I want to honor you because of who you are in my life. I pray that you continue to reveal yourself to me in different ways. I thank you for wanting to speak to us. Please help us to remember you are God alone, and no one could ever take your place in Jesus's/ Yeshua's name, Amen.

Elimination Station:

_____
_____
_____
_____
_____
_____
_____
_____

Day 14

Loneliness Verses Being Alone

<u>*Scripture:*</u> "The Lord himself goes before you and will be with you; he will never leave you nor forsake you. Do not be afraid; do not be discouraged." ***Deuteronomy 31:8 NIV***

Testimony:

I used to be afraid of the dark, but as I got older, I grew out of that. After a while, I found myself fearful of being alone. I battled with these thoughts in all areas of my life. I feared that either something would happen to me and no one would be around to help me or that I would die alone, never having the experience of true love. These thoughts took over my mind until I evaluated my life. I realized I have always had people who loved me and cared for me, but what do you do when loneliness has been deceiving you all this time.

My perspective changed at that moment. I would sometimes feel alone in a crowded room of loved ones because loneliness would have me believe I needed love in a certain way or from certain people to make me feel secure. Loneliness is the actual emotion of sadness or abandonment that we feel when things do not work out how we think they should go. To be alone is the state of isolation or solitude away from others. There is a big difference between loneliness and being alone. Being alone is healthy sometimes because it gives us a chance to reset, think about life, get to know ourselves, or even gather our thoughts. I had to surrender my fears & expectations of people to God in order to be free from loneliness. God revealed to me that He has always been with me and will never leave me because He loves me that much. Remember, God loves us all, and He promised us that He would never leave us. He is our comfort and always willing to hold us close when we need it. Let loneliness go and embrace being alone at times because God is with you.

Prayer:

Sovereign Lord,

I want to thank you for your love and your promises. Help us to realize you are always there even if we can't see you all the time. Strip us of loneliness so it will no longer deceive our minds. Continue to embrace us in our weak moments in Jesus's/ Yeshua's name, Amen.

Elimination Station:

_____
_____
_____
_____
_____
_____
_____
_____

Day 15

If You Judge It, You Will Become It

Scripture: "For in the same way you judge others, you will be judged, and with the measure you use, it will be measured to you." *Matthew 7:2 NIV*

Testimony:

If we do not righteously judge according to the lead of the Spirit of God, we will become what we think is wrong because it will consume our mind. We must allow God to refocus our perspective so we can see things as He sees them. We tend to be quick to judge people, places, and things we do not understand instead of seeking God first on the revelation of the matter. Even when we see things that are out of order, we should pray on behalf of the situation so God can intervene and make it right. In my experience, I have been a judge and have even judged others with no understanding of their situation.

Every action has a reaction, and we may never understand the action that caused the things we see. We have to make sure we have ourselves in order, so God does not rain judgment on us. God's ruling does not compare to anyone else's because God holds life and death in His hands. It is time for us to fully follow God's commands and even love one another no matter what.

Prayer:

Lord,

Please help us to be more understanding and patient with one another. Show us when we need to be on the wall of prayer for our brothers and sisters in Jesus Christ. Forgive us when we were harsh and judgmental to each other instead of lending a helping hand in Jesus's/ Yeshua's name, Amen.

Elimination Station:

_____
_____
_____
_____
_____
_____
_____
_____
_____

Day 16

I Am A Perfectionist, And It Drives Me Crazy

> *Scripture:* "Whatever you do, work at it with all your heart, as working for the Lord, not for human masters," **Colossians 3:23 NIV**

Testimony:

I consider myself a helpful person. I pride myself on making sure everything is picture-perfect. This picture could include people, places, or things. I would push past limits to make certain perfection was mastered except to accomplish something for myself. I found myself drained by the time I thought to include assignments. I do find joy in caring for other's needs before mines. Sometimes I ask myself should there be a cutoff point? I have realized that the more I give, the more others need.

I began to seek God for strength every day because an overload of assignments would consistently track me down. God revealed to me that I was going about everything wrong! He began to show me that although I was doing a good thing, it was not a right. He said I was being nice to others, but my motives were not in the right place. I was doing these good deeds to satisfy myself and others, but not seeking God to see what He wanted of me. I was taking on assignments that God never intended for me to handle. I extended myself to the people as if I was God. In turn, the people would run to me for a quick fix to perfect a problem instead of seeking God.

I had taken God's place by standing in His way and did not even realize it. I thought I was helping the people, but I was only crippling them. I was even causing damage to myself and everyone around me. We must realize that God does not need our help, but He wants to use us. He assigns us to specific assignments that He equip us for, and He gives us the strength to get through them. We cannot save the world because His son, Jesus Christ has already done that. When we are a perfectionist, we are blinded by how we think things should be and that is a recipe for disaster. God is in control and has the first, middle, and final saying about all things. I had to surrender trying to be all things to all people because that is God's job alone. Once I did that I was not drained, tired, had time for family & myself. Allow God to lead you where He wants you to be and who He wants you to assist.

Prayer:

Lord God,

Forgive me for standing in your way. I give myself and your people back to you to do what you want to do. I know now that you can help us better than I can any day. I thank you for taking on the responsibility of caring for us each day. Thank you for creating us and knowing just what we need at all times in Jesus's/ Yeshua's name, Amen.

Elimination Station:

_____
_____
_____
_____
_____
_____
_____

Day 17

The Healing Begins Now

Scripture: "And he said, "Who told you that you were naked? Have you eaten from the tree that I commanded you not to eat from?" ***Genesis 3:11 NIV***

Testimony:

When I entered the business world, I realized there was so much that I did not know. I would sit in the back of the room so no one would call on me for my input. I did not want them to realize how unlearned I was in this area. Yes, I knew some basics to get me into the room, but when I compared myself to the others, I was at the bottom of the list. I did not like to feel inadequate because I was used to being the smart one in a room. I started to doubt myself feeling like I was not smart enough to even sit in the room. Fear walked in and had a conversation with me; in turn, I wanted to give up everything. I had just started to get clients inquiring about my business, but I thought I would not be the best fit for them.

I would put these thoughts in the back of my mind every day, but my joy and peace of mind were gone. I was excited to become a business owner at first, only wanting to close the doors now. I went on like this for months until a friend pointed out that they noticed a shift in my desire for my company. I knew at this point only God could change this mess that I had encountered.

Once I got into prayer, God showed me details of my life. I had seen how there were cycles similar to this situation. I would have moments where I would be doing great in life, and then thoughts would take over and set me back. I had to ask God why these thoughts were haunting me and where they were coming from. Was it me? God revealed that I had some things in my childhood and even adulthood that I did not confront. Instead, I concealed it all, not wanting to face it. I created more wounds on top of an injury, and the wounds continued to grow over the years.

I may not be the smartest one in every room, but that was only the surface issue. It was more profound than that, which caused roots to grow and create cycles in my life. When I was younger, and even in adult relationships, I was mentally and emotionally abused. I was rarely commended for anything. I was overlooked and barely appreciated. I carried this pain for years until I forgot, sweeping it under the rug. I noticed I would beat myself down before anyone else could, and then I would be quick to give up. I had already adopted the mindset that no one would care about what I accomplished, and it was poisoning the great things I did and wanted to do. It created doubt and fear of the unknown.

Today was my breaking point. No longer could I go on like this. I asked God to erase everything negative that would prevent me from moving forward, cycles included. I had to forgive all of those who hurt me and release them to God. God changed my perspective about my imperfections, and now I can sit in any room no matter if I know it all or not. He placed me in certain places to gain knowledge and understanding from others to master new areas. We are all pieces of God's puzzle that fit together. No one person is the whole puzzle, so be okay with learning something new. Don't allow anything to stop your growth, not even yourself.

Prayer:

Dear Lord,

I thank you for your revelation of life. I thank you for breaking chains and cycles off your people. Please help us forgive and even forgive us when we hold on to pain, fear, and doubt. Show us which beautiful puzzle piece we are in your eyes in Jesus's/ Yeshua's name, Amen.

Elimination Station:

_____
_____
_____
_____
_____

Day 18

Location Is Everything

Scripture: "He said, "Throw your net on the right side of the boat and you will find some." When they did, they were unable to haul the net in because of the large number of fish." ***John 21:6 NIV***

Testimony:

I remember looking for a house that would accommodate my entire family. We are a big family that has a bunch of different needs. Space and location were one of our priorities. We spent some much time living on top of each other that it drove us crazy. Yes, we love each other, but sometimes a break was needed. The location we lived in was high crime, and the kids could not safely play outside. We needed to relocate! We looked all over the city, trying to find a house in a nice neighborhood, a good school, and within our budget. Months of searching and working on our credit with no breakthrough made us want to give up. We knew we were at our limits where we lived, but what to do?

The good neighborhoods with bigger homes were out of our price range. We worked jobs living paycheck to paycheck. We listened to the advice of everyone, including the things we thought of, but nothing worked! We were in the same place doing the same things. I finally got tired of it and began to seek God with everything I had inside of me. He showed me it was not about our expertise, credit, money, or plans. He told me it was about Him changing our perspective towards the issue. We can do everything we think is correct, but until we do it God's way, we will go in circles.

I asked God to show me what we needed to do, and He gave me a city in another state to look up properties. We were scared because we had never been there. God wanted us to shift in another direction. He wanted us out of our comfort zone, totally depending on Him alone! Once we let go of fear, we did some research and met with a landlord. After the first meeting, the rest was history. The landlord showed us favor beyond anything we could ever imagine. The house was everything we needed in a nice neighborhood and with a good school. He did not require a credit check, nor did he care about how much income we had. He just asked if we could make the payments every month, and our "yes" was good enough for him. He even allowed us time to come up with the deposit and closed the deal that day so no one else could make an offer.

That was one of the happiest moments in my life. I have seen God do a lot for my family and me, and I am forever grateful. When you follow God's instructions, there is no limit to what He can do in your life. Get out of the mindset that the world made us believe the only way and trust God. He knows what you need, when you need it and where you need to be. The saying is true, "you have to be in the right place at the right time."

Prayer:

Father God,

We would be grateful if you could download your wisdom, knowledge, and understanding to us so we can live according to your will for our lives. Father, please forgive us every time we followed our direction, knowledge, and others. Please show us the location you want us and guide us every step of the way in Jesus's/Yeshua's name, Amen.

Elimination Station:

_____
_____
_____
_____
_____
_____
_____

Day 19

The Why Over the What

Scripture: "So I find this law at work: Although I want to do good, evil is right there with me." ***Romans 7:21 NIV***

Testimony:

As I turned on the radio, melodies from the past swept the station. I could not believe I heard old jams from a well-known artist that my children enjoyed. They would play these songs over and over, getting on my nerves until one day I gave in, and they grew on me. I would hear this artist's music everywhere.

I turned to another station, and they were playing the same artist! Maybe it was a coincidence until I turned on the television, and the news stations were covering a story on the same artist. I went to social media for the latest tea (news/gossip), and there were reports that the artist was dead! He died of a heart attack and possible overdose of drugs. I could not believe what I was reading, but it all made sense after witnessing all the attention on the artist.

Everyone had mixed emotions about whether to celebrate his accomplishments or not. Some believed that he knew God, so it permitted them to honor him despite the music he produced and the life he lived. He created music that glorified the rap & motorcycle world, diminished women's values, killing, etc. Through his music, he also gave us a glimpse of his life. His life was dark, according to some tracks he wrote. I always wondered what made people write, sing, rap, etc., about the topics they chose. I guess I began to understand when I became a writer.

When I write, I feel free to be me. I share life experiences and even observations that I have witnessed. I am sure that is what this artist did. To hear some people talk bad about him because of the life he chose to live even after becoming big with his music career had me thinking. Yes, he did drugs, drank, had multiple children with multiple women. He was married today then divorced tomorrow. He seemed confused and all over the place making decisions. He had lawsuits and even went bankrupt trying to support his drug habit. He was mentally unstable but possibly could've been a nice guy. In no way do I agree with the way he chose to live his life or want to argue about his salvation, but I do want us to start looking deeper into people's behavior.

On the surface, he was a mess, but what was going on within? Why was this behavior going on? How did he get to this point in life? It turns out that the artist went through a lot growing up, from being molested, abused, abandoned, rejected, and neglected. Some of which was at the hands of his mother. His father walked out, and he had to look after himself. His grandmother tried to help him out as much as she could until she died. Then he went off the deep end of life. I know it doesn't take away from the fact that he chose his way to deal with issues, but why not be compassionate and understanding like Jesus? Jesus extended himself to everyone with love and kindness even if He found them in their mess of sin. He knows we all fall short every single day, hence why He gave Himself up for us. If we had it all together, we would not need Him. If it had not been for Jesus, I would still be stuck in all the mess I was able to overcome!

Let's stop criticizing others because of what they struggle with. Their struggle may not be yours, but we all struggle with something. No one sin is greater than the next. The Bible tells us the wages for all sin is death. I thank God every day for His son, Jesus, because He died for our sins, so we now have the opportunity to be forgiven and saved from death. Extend the olive branch of mercy and grace to one another even if you know of their sins. The Word of God says to confess our sins one to another and pray for each other so we may be healed. We hear each other's sins and immediately write people off instead of praying for them! There is no healing taking place, so we are stuck going in circles of sin. Yes, we choose certain issues, but some issues choose us.

In conclusion, let us be more understanding of each other. I am not saying accept their sin, but love and pray them through it. When we are honest with our "why" (mess), we can be delivered from our "what" (roots of issue).

Prayer:

God,

Please help your people out of the mess that they created for themselves. I pray that we become more compassionate towards one another. Show us how to pull each other out of the darkness with your love and kindness in Jesus's/Yeshua's name, Amen.

Elimination Station:

_____
_____
_____
_____
_____
_____
_____
_____

Day 20

I Am Free

Scripture: "So if the Son sets you free, you will be free indeed."
John 8:36 NIV

Testimony:

I will never forget I met this guy at a nightclub. I thought he was incredible, and perhaps we could have built a future together. We started hanging out and getting close. He would spend the night at my house now and then. We formed a relationship that seemed to be going well until I stayed over at his house one night! I noticed his place was set up like a jail cell. I thought maybe he just needed help decorating or something. Jokingly I asked him why he had me in prison? He did not find it funny. He confessed that he had been locked up for some time before. The way he lived outside of his home, I would have never guessed that. His house, on the other hand, gave it away. He had his bed made up like a prison bunk. The ironing board was out with parchment paper to prepare a grilled cheese sandwich with the iron. A clothing line hung across the room with pictures hanging from it that he drew. He had a prayer rug in the corner and even took a break to pray for a while. His clothes were even folded weirdly, so I just assumed the prison taught him that as well.

I did not have a problem with him going to jail in the past, but I was concerned about his present and future living conditions. He had been physically released from prison but still carried the prison mentality home every night. It was almost like he restructured his house to match the prison so he could feel comfortable. Which in turn told me that he was comfortable being in prison, and it was still a part of him. I knew this was not the life I wanted to live, so I had to part ways with him. It's one thing to be physically free, but if you are not willing to be mentally free, you will remain stuck. Him getting out of prison is freedom, but "Indeed" freedom is when the prison is out of him!

The son of God, Jesus, set us free when He laid down His life for us. That is the picture of "indeed" freedom! We will not get any freer than that! When Jesus does a thing, His stamp of approval signs it as a done deal. We have to receive it and walk in it. The mind is truly a terrible thing to waste, so exchange yours with The Lord today. I promise you there is nothing to lose except the warden that holds you hostage.

Prayer:

Dear Lord,

I can not thank you enough for your "indeed" freedom. I pray that all your people will experience your "indeed" freedom in their lives. Please save them from the battles that take over their mind in Jesus's/Yeshua's name, Amen.

Elimination Station:

_____
_____
_____
_____
_____
_____
_____
_____

Day 21

You Are A Survivor

Scripture: "No, in all these things, we are more than conquerors through him who loved us." **Romans 8:37 NIV**

Testimony:

July 2020, I discovered a lump in my left breast. I made a doctor's appointment because it was painful. The area was sensitive to touch and was only getting worst. When I got to the doctor's appointment, they told me they were not too worried because it was impossible to be cancer. They claimed cancer did not hurt. However, I continued to complain about the pain, so they scheduled an ultrasound and a mammogram. The ultrasound did not show good signs; therefore, the doctor scheduled a biopsy to test a piece of the problem tissue. I am nervous and scared because the last word I want to hear is "cancer!" I have been through cancer before and beat it, but it took a lot out of me. Cancer even took several people I knew. I prayed around the clock and held onto my faith because that was all I had.

Seven days later, I got the results back, and it was stage three breast cancer! I was devasted. I could not believe what I was hearing. I cried out to God, asking Him why this again, only to get no response. I began chemo treatment in August. I did sixteen rounds, to be exact. I do not wish that on my worst enemy because I suffered greatly through the process. I felt as if I had already died. I was waiting to hear the voice of The Lord. I was sick every day. I felt weak, unhappy, depressed, suicidal, neglected, and abandoned. My hair fell out, my feet and hands turned black, and my nails looked like they belonged to an animal. I gained weight having to buy a whole new wardrobe. I felt so unattractive! I was used to dressing nice and feeling good about myself, but it was exhausting fighting the downward spiral of the chemo treatment process. I tried to keep the faith every moment, hoping that God would heal me instantly. That was not the case for me.

I finished the final chemo treatment on January 11, 2021. February 15, 2021, they took the chip out of my chest that they installed when they did the first biopsy. My follow-up appointment was on February 24, 2021, and I did not know what to expect. I received so many reports from different doctors, but all I wanted to know was when it would end? I was tired of the routine visits only to feel like I was going in circles. I never stopped praying and believing that I would be healed. If He did it before, He surely could do it again. As I waited for the doctor to step into the room, every thought possible ran through my mind. The doctor entered with a smile, giving me some relief. To my fulfillment, the doctor announced that I was cancer-free! She said she could not even find a trace.

Tears of joy flowed uncontrollably. I did not know what to do at that moment. I wanted to run, scream, speak in tongues, call everyone in my contacts, but the one thing I did do was shout Hallelujah! I owned God all of the glory because, without Him, I would not even be here to tell the story. I am grateful for life, my health, and the strength to go on. Day 21 is special to me because I survived it! It is not so much about surviving cancer but about everything that came with it. I went through hell and back, trying not to lose my mind. I am happy that God is a keeper!

No matter what you are going through, hold on to your faith. You, too, can survive whatever issue you are facing. If God kept me, He could keep you too.

Prayer:

Heavenly God,

I honor you for who you are. I thank you for keeping me. I thank you for healing and saving me. I even thank you for being The Healer for your people. There's honestly nobody like you. I searched a significant number of places, and still, I have found no one like you. Thank you for your breathe of life that runs through my body. I owe you my life. Please continue to show yourself might in your people's lives In Jesus's/ Yeshua's name, Amen.

Elimination Station:

_____
_____
_____
_____
_____
_____
_____
_____
_____

www.ingramcontent.com/pod-product-compliance
Lightning Source LLC
Chambersburg PA
CBHW072040080526
44578CB00007B/539